GRATITUDE

30 days to an enlightened heart, mind and soul

My Journal

and Daily Planner

Acknowledging the good that you already have in your life, is the foundation for all abundance.
~ Eckhart Tolle

Repetition creates a habit. I encourage you to take the time to fill out each day with intention.

Use the journal pages to leave any negative feelings from the day behind as you move on to gratitude and reflection.

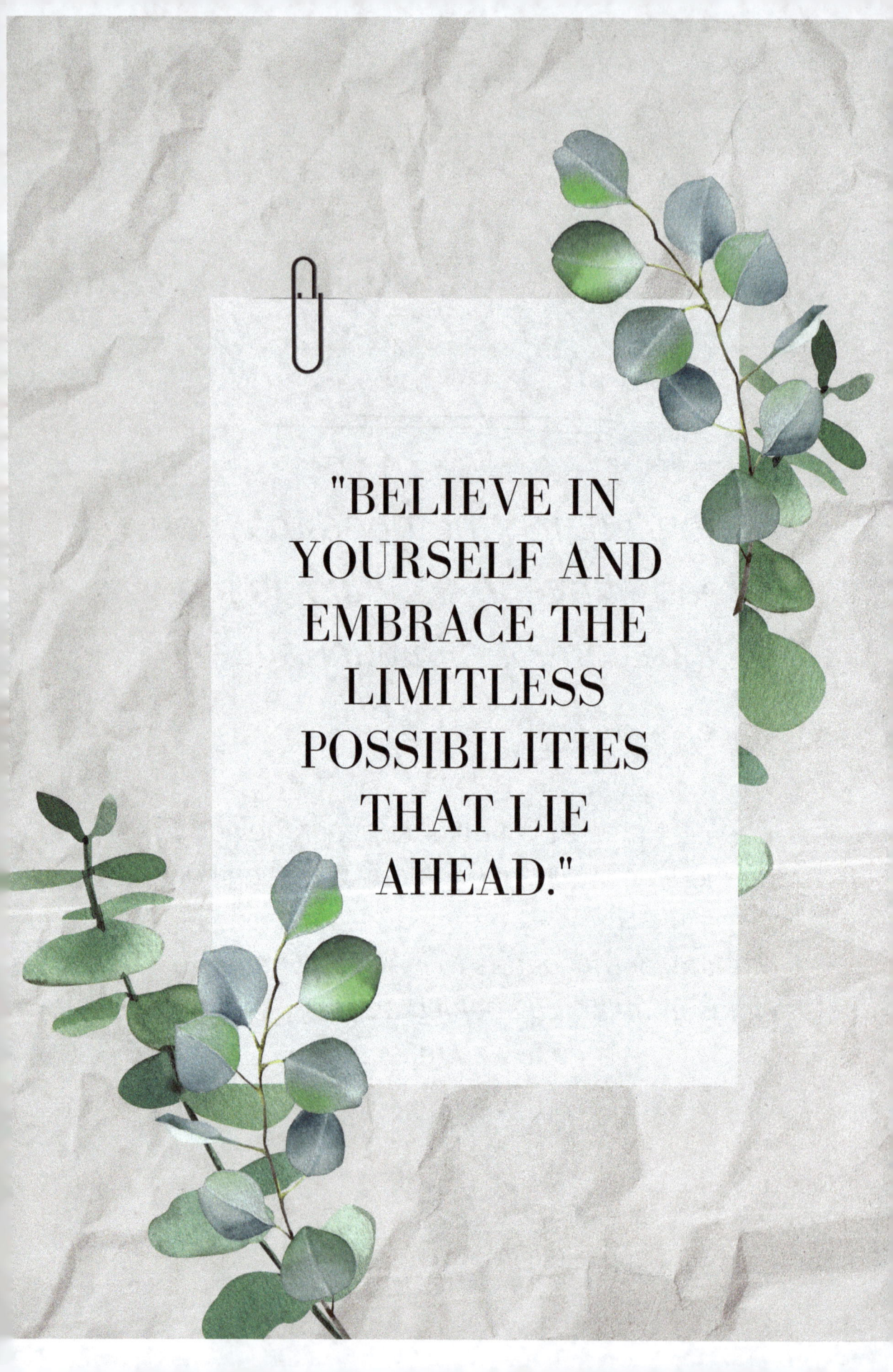

"BELIEVE IN YOURSELF AND EMBRACE THE LIMITLESS POSSIBILITIES THAT LIE AHEAD."

Morning Gratitude

Date: _____

Today I want to feel...

_____
_____
_____

Today I will spread kindness by...

_____
_____
_____

3 things I'm grateful for today are...

_____
_____
_____

"Happiness is a habit."

To Do List

- ○ _____
- ○ _____
- ○ _____
- ○ _____
- ○ _____
- ○ _____
- ○ _____
- ○ _____

Goals

For Tomorrow

Notes

_____
_____
_____
_____
_____
_____
_____

Daily Journal

Evening Gratitude

3 things I'm grateful for today are...

_____

_____

_____

The best part of today was...

_____

_____

_____

What can I learn from today's experiences?

_____

_____

_____

Tomorrow I'm looking forward to...

_____

_____

_____

"Do more of what you love."

Morning Gratitude

Date: _____

Today I want to feel...

_____
_____
_____

Today I will spread kindness by...

_____
_____
_____

3 things I'm grateful for today are...

_____
_____
_____

Meditate, relax and just "be" for a
moment. Remember that this moment
is perfect the way it is and you don't
need to change it.
~Maxime Lagacé

To Do List

- ○ _____
- ○ _____
- ○ _____
- ○ _____
- ○ _____
- ○ _____
- ○ _____
- ○ _____

Goals

For Tomorrow

Notes

Daily Journal

_____

_____

_____

_____

_____

_____

_____

_____

_____

_____

_____

_____

_____

_____

_____

_____

_____

_____

_____

_____

_____

Evening Gratitude

3 things I'm grateful for today are...

_____

_____

_____

The best part of today was...

_____

_____

_____

What can I learn from today's experiences?

_____

_____

_____

Tomorrow I'm looking forward to...

_____

_____

_____

Gratitude is what you feel when you
want what you already have.
~James Clear

Morning Gratitude

Date: _____

Today I want to feel...

_____

_____

_____

Today I will spread kindness by...

_____

_____

_____

3 things I'm grateful for today are...

_____

_____

_____

The world gives you way more than
you ever give it.
~Kamal Ravikant

Wednesday

To Do List

- ○ _____
- ○ _____
- ○ _____
- ○ _____
- ○ _____
- ○ _____
- ○ _____
- ○ _____

Goals

For Tomorrow

Notes

_____
_____
_____
_____
_____
_____

Daily Journal

_____

_____

_____

_____

_____

_____

_____

_____

_____

_____

_____

_____

_____

_____

_____

_____

_____

_____

_____

_____

_____

_____

Evening Gratitude

3 things I'm grateful for today are...

_____

_____

_____

The best part of today was...

_____

_____

_____

What can I learn from today's experiences?

_____

_____

_____

Tomorrow I'm looking forward to...

_____

_____

_____

Give thanks for a little and you will
find a lot.
~Hansa proverb

Morning Gratitude

Date: _____

Today I want to feel...

_____
_____
_____

Today I will spread kindness by...

_____
_____
_____

3 things I'm grateful for today are...

_____
_____
_____

Gratitude turns what we have
into enough.
~Aesop

To Do List

- ○ _____
- ○ _____
- ○ _____
- ○ _____
- ○ _____
- ○ _____
- ○ _____
- ○ _____

Goals

For Tomorrow

Notes

_____
_____
_____
_____
_____

Daily Journal

_____

_____

_____

_____

_____

_____

_____

_____

_____

_____

_____

_____

_____

_____

_____

_____

_____

_____

_____

_____

_____

Evening Gratitude

3 things I'm grateful for today are...

_____

_____

_____

The best part of today was...

_____

_____

_____

What can I learn from today's experiences?

_____

_____

_____

Tomorrow I'm looking forward to...

_____

_____

_____

The real gift of gratitude is that the
more grateful you are, the more
present you become.
~ Robert Holden

Morning Gratitude

Date: _____

Today I want to feel...

_____

_____

_____

Today I will spread kindness by...

_____

_____

_____

3 things I'm grateful for today are...

_____

_____

_____

It's not easy being grateful all the time.
But it's when you feel least thankful that
you are most in need of what gratitude
can give you.
~ Oprah Winfrey

To Do List

- ○ _____
- ○ _____
- ○ _____
- ○ _____
- ○ _____
- ○ _____
- ○ _____
- ○ _____

Goals

For Tomorrow

Notes

_____
_____
_____
_____
_____
_____

Daily Journal

_____

_____

_____

_____

_____

_____

_____

_____

_____

_____

_____

_____

_____

_____

_____

_____

_____

_____

_____

_____

Evening Gratitude

3 things I'm grateful for today are...

_____
_____
_____

The best part of today was...

_____
_____
_____

What can I learn from today's experiences?

_____
_____
_____

Tomorrow I'm looking forward to...

_____
_____

The more grateful you are, the more
your life overflows with abundance.
~ Lailah Gifty Akita

Morning Gratitude

Date: _____

Today I want to feel...

_____
_____
_____

Today I will spread kindness by...

_____
_____
_____

3 things I'm grateful for today are...

_____
_____
_____

To be thankful for one thing is
infinitely more powerful than to be
bitter about a hundred others.
~Craig D. Lounsbrough

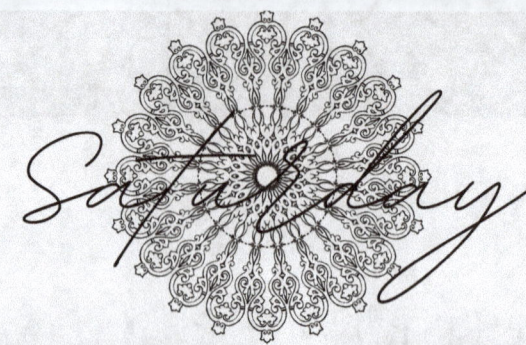

To Do List

- ○ _____
- ○ _____
- ○ _____
- ○ _____
- ○ _____
- ○ _____
- ○ _____
- ○ _____

Goals

For Tomorrow

Notes

Daily Journal

_____
_____
_____
_____
_____
_____
_____
_____
_____
_____
_____
_____
_____
_____
_____
_____
_____
_____
_____
_____
_____

Evening Gratitude

3 things I'm grateful for today are...

_____

_____

_____

The best part of today was...

_____

_____

_____

What can I learn from today's experiences?

_____

_____

_____

Tomorrow I'm looking forward to...

_____

_____

_____

Gratitude is not just about being thankful
for the good things in our life; it is about
being thankful for everything in our life.
-Nadine Sadaka Boulos

Morning Gratitude

Date: _____

Today I want to feel...

_____

_____

_____

Today I will spread kindness by...

_____

_____

_____

3 things I'm grateful for today are...

_____

_____

_____

You ought to be thankful a whole
heaping lot. for the places and
people you're lucky you're not!
~Dr. Suess

To Do List

- ○ _____
- ○ _____
- ○ _____
- ○ _____
- ○ _____
- ○ _____
- ○ _____
- ○ _____

Goals

For Tomorrow

Notes

_____
_____
_____
_____
_____
_____

Daily Journal

_____
_____
_____
_____
_____
_____
_____
_____
_____
_____
_____
_____
_____
_____
_____
_____
_____
_____
_____

Evening Gratitude

3 things I'm grateful for today are...

_____

_____

_____

The best part of today was...

_____

_____

_____

What can I learn from today's experiences?

_____

_____

_____

Tomorrow I'm looking forward to...

_____

_____

_____

The thankful heart opens our eyes to a
multitude of blessings that
continually surround us.
~James E. Faust

Weekly check in

DATE _____

TOP 3 THINGS I DID THIS WEEK

○ _____

○ _____

○ _____

MOST REWARDING INTERACTION I HAD THIS WEEK

THIS WEEK I FELT

NEXT WEEK I WANT TO

_____

_____

_____

_____

THINGS I ACCOMPLISHED THIS WEEK

WHAT WAS THE BEST THING ABOUT THE WEEK?

MY RANKING OF THE WEEK

☆ ☆ ☆ ☆ ☆

GENTLE REMINDER

TAKE A DEEP BREATH

TREAT PEOPLE WITH KINDNESS

TELL YOURSELF THAT EVERYTHING WILL BE OKAY

DO THE BEST YOU CAN

Morning Gratitude

Date: _____

Today I want to feel...

_____
_____
_____

Today I will spread kindness by...

_____
_____
_____

3 things I'm grateful for today are...

_____
_____
_____

We can complain because rose bushes
have thorns. or rejoice because thorns
have roses.
~Alphonse Karr

Monday

To Do List

- ○ _____
- ○ _____
- ○ _____
- ○ _____
- ○ _____
- ○ _____
- ○ _____
- ○ _____

Goals

For Tomorrow

Notes

_____
_____
_____
_____
_____
_____
_____

Daily Journal

_____

_____

_____

_____

_____

_____

_____

_____

_____

_____

_____

_____

_____

_____

_____

_____

_____

_____

_____

Evening Gratitude

3 things I'm grateful for today are...

_____

_____

_____

The best part of today was...

_____

_____

_____

What can I learn from today's experiences?

_____

_____

_____

Tomorrow I'm looking forward to...

_____

_____

_____

Be blessed. The simple things are also
the most extraordinary things, and only
the wise can see them.
~Paulo Coelho

Morning Gratitude

Date: _____

Today I want to feel...

_____
_____
_____

Today I will spread kindness by...

_____
_____
_____
_____

3 things I'm grateful for today are...

_____
_____
_____

I learned a long time ago, the wisest
thing I can do is be on my own
side."
- Maya Angelou

Tuesday

To Do List

- ◯ _____
- ◯ _____
- ◯ _____
- ◯ _____
- ◯ _____
- ◯ _____
- ◯ _____
- ◯ _____

Goals

For Tomorrow

Notes

_____
_____
_____
_____
_____

Daily Journal

_____

_____

_____

_____

_____

_____

_____

_____

_____

_____

_____

_____

_____

_____

_____

_____

_____

_____

_____

Evening Gratitude

3 things I'm grateful for today are...

_____

_____

_____

The best part of today was...

_____

_____

_____

What can I learn from today's experiences?

_____

_____

_____

Tomorrow I'm looking forward to...

_____

_____

_____

Let us rise up and be thankful, for if we didn't learn a
lot today, at least we learned a little, and if we didn't
learn a little, at least we didn't get sick, and if we got
sick, at least we didn't die; so, let us all be thankful.
-Buddha

Morning Gratitude

Date: _____

Today I want to feel...

_____

_____

_____

Today I will spread kindness by...

_____

_____

_____

3 things I'm grateful for today are...

_____

_____

_____

True forgiveness is when you can
say. "Thank you for that experience".
~Oprah Winfrey

Wednesday

To Do List

- ○ _____
- ○ _____
- ○ _____
- ○ _____
- ○ _____
- ○ _____
- ○ _____
- ○ _____

Goals

For Tomorrow

Notes

_____
_____
_____
_____
_____
_____

Daily Journal

Evening Gratitude

3 things I'm grateful for today are...

_____

_____

_____

The best part of today was...

_____

_____

_____

What can I learn from today's experiences?

_____

_____

_____

Tomorrow I'm looking forward to...

_____

_____

_____

What separates privilege from
entitlement is gratitude.
-Brené Brown

Morning Gratitude

Date: _____

Today I want to feel...

_____

_____

_____

Today I will spread kindness by...

_____

_____

_____

3 things I'm grateful for today are...

_____

_____

_____

When gratitude becomes an essential
foundation in our lives, miracles start to
appear everywhere.
- Emmanuel Dagher

To Do List

- ○ _____
- ○ _____
- ○ _____
- ○ _____
- ○ _____
- ○ _____
- ○ _____
- ○ _____

Goals

For Tomorrow

Notes

_____
_____
_____
_____
_____

Daily Journal

_____

_____

_____

_____

_____

_____

_____

_____

_____

_____

_____

_____

_____

_____

_____

_____

_____

_____

_____

_____

_____

_____

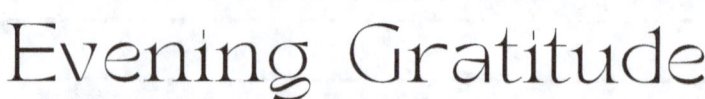

Evening Gratitude

3 things I'm grateful for today are...

_____

_____

_____

The best part of today was...

_____

_____

What can I learn from today's experiences?

_____

_____

Tomorrow I'm looking forward to...

_____

_____

When you are grateful, fear
disappears and abundance appears.
-Tony Robbins

Morning Gratitude

Date: _____

Today I want to feel...

_____

_____

_____

Today I will spread kindness by...

_____

_____

_____

3 things I'm grateful for today are...

_____

_____

_____

There are always flowers for
those who want to see them.
~Henri Matisse

To Do List

- ○ _____
- ○ _____
- ○ _____
- ○ _____
- ○ _____
- ○ _____
- ○ _____
- ○ _____

Goals

For Tomorrow

Notes

_____
_____
_____
_____
_____
_____

Daily Journal

_____

_____

_____

_____

_____

_____

_____

_____

_____

_____

_____

_____

_____

_____

_____

_____

_____

_____

Evening Gratitude

3 things I'm grateful for today are...

_____
_____
_____

The best part of today was...

_____
_____
_____

What can I learn from today's experiences?

_____
_____
_____

Tomorrow I'm looking forward to...

_____
_____
_____

Wear gratitude like a cloak and it will
feed every corner of your life.
~Rumi

Morning Gratitude

Date: _____

Today I want to feel...

_____
_____
_____

Today I will spread kindness by...

_____
_____
_____

3 things I'm grateful for today are...

_____
_____
_____

Appreciation is the purest vibration
that exists on the planet today.
~Abraham Hicks

To Do List

- _____
- _____
- _____
- _____
- _____
- _____
- _____
- _____

Goals

For Tomorrow

Notes

_____
_____
_____
_____
_____

Daily Journal

Evening Gratitude

3 things I'm grateful for today are...

_____
_____
_____

The best part of today was...

_____
_____
_____

What can I learn from today's experiences?

_____
_____
_____

Tomorrow I'm looking forward to...

_____
_____
_____

Three meals plus bedtime make four
sure blessings a day.
~Mason Cooley

Morning Gratitude

Date: _____

Today I want to feel...

_____
_____
_____

Today I will spread kindness by...

_____
_____
_____

3 things I'm grateful for today are...

_____
_____
_____

If you count all your assets, you
always show a profit.
~Robert Quillen

To Do List

- ○ _____
- ○ _____
- ○ _____
- ○ _____
- ○ _____
- ○ _____
- ○ _____
- ○ _____

Goals

For Tomorrow

Notes

_____
_____
_____
_____
_____
_____

Daily Journal

_____

_____

_____

_____

_____

_____

_____

_____

_____

_____

_____

_____

_____

_____

_____

_____

_____

_____

_____

_____

_____

_____

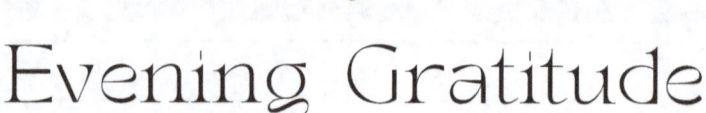

Evening Gratitude

3 things I'm grateful for today are...

_____

_____

_____

The best part of today was...

_____

_____

_____

What can I learn from today's experiences?

_____

_____

_____

Tomorrow I'm looking forward to...

_____

_____

_____

It's not happiness that brings us gratitude.
It's gratitude that brings us happiness.
~Jeremiah Say

Weekly check in

DATE _____

TOP 3 THINGS I DID THIS WEEK

○ _____

○ _____

○ _____

THIS WEEK I FELT

NEXT WEEK I WANT TO

_____

_____

_____

_____

MOST REWARDING INTERACTION I HAD THIS WEEK

THINGS I ACCOMPLISHED THIS WEEK

WHAT WAS THE BEST THING ABOUT THE WEEK?

MY RANKING OF THE WEEK

☆ ☆ ☆ ☆ ☆

> You have the power to protect your peace.

Morning Gratitude

Date: _____

Today I want to feel...

_____
_____
_____

Today I will spread kindness by...

_____
_____
_____

3 things I'm grateful for today are...

_____
_____
_____

Not what we say about our blessings,
but how we use them, is the true
measure of our thanksgiving.
~W.T. Purkiser

To Do List

- ○ _____
- ○ _____
- ○ _____
- ○ _____
- ○ _____
- ○ _____
- ○ _____
- ○ _____

Goals

For Tomorrow

Notes

Daily Journal

_____

_____

_____

_____

_____

_____

_____

_____

_____

_____

_____

_____

_____

_____

_____

_____

_____

_____

Evening Gratitude

3 things I'm grateful for today are...

_____

_____

_____

The best part of today was...

_____

_____

_____

What can I learn from today's experiences?

_____

_____

_____

Tomorrow I'm looking forward to...

_____

_____

_____

Appreciation is a wonderful thing. It
makes what is excellent in others belong
to us as well.
~Voltaire

Morning Gratitude

Date: _____

Today I want to feel...

_____
_____
_____

Today I will spread kindness by...

_____
_____
_____

3 things I'm grateful for today are...

_____
_____
_____

Gratitude can transform common days into
thanksgivings, turn routine jobs into joy,
and change ordinary opportunities into
blessings.
~William Arthur Ward

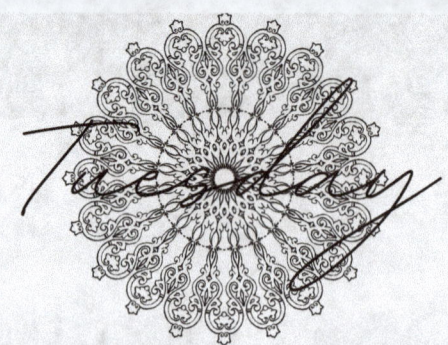

To Do List

- ○ _____
- ○ _____
- ○ _____
- ○ _____
- ○ _____
- ○ _____
- ○ _____
- ○ _____

Goals

For Tomorrow

Notes

Daily Journal

_____

_____

_____

_____

_____

_____

_____

_____

_____

_____

_____

_____

_____

_____

_____

_____

_____

_____

_____

_____

_____

_____

Evening Gratitude

3 things I'm grateful for today are...

_____

_____

_____

The best part of today was...

_____

_____

_____

What can I learn from today's experiences?

_____

_____

_____

Tomorrow I'm looking forward to...

_____

_____

_____

What may seem a curse may be a
blessing, and what may be a blessing
may be a curse.
~Muso Kokushi

Morning Gratitude

Date: _____

Today I want to feel...

_____

_____

_____

Today I will spread kindness by...

_____

_____

_____

3 things I'm grateful for today are...

_____

_____

_____

If the only prayer you said in your
whole life was "thank you"
that would suffice.
~Eckhart Tolle

To Do List

- ○ _____
- ○ _____
- ○ _____
- ○ _____
- ○ _____
- ○ _____
- ○ _____
- ○ _____

Goals

For Tomorrow

Notes

Daily Journal

Evening Gratitude

3 things I'm grateful for today are...

_____

_____

_____

The best part of today was...

_____

_____

_____

What can I learn from today's experiences?

_____

_____

_____

Tomorrow I'm looking forward to...

_____

_____

_____

Gratitude is riches.
Complaint is poverty.
-Doris Day

Morning Gratitude

Date: _____

Today I want to feel...

_____

_____

_____

Today I will spread kindness by...

_____

_____

_____

3 things I'm grateful for today are...

_____

_____

_____

An early-morning walk is a
blessing for the whole day.
~Henry David Thoreau

Thursday

To Do List

- ○ _____
- ○ _____
- ○ _____
- ○ _____
- ○ _____
- ○ _____
- ○ _____
- ○ _____

Goals

For Tomorrow

Notes

Daily Journal

_____

_____

_____

_____

_____

_____

_____

_____

_____

_____

_____

_____

_____

_____

_____

_____

_____

_____

_____

_____

_____

Evening Gratitude

3 things I'm grateful for today are...

_____

_____

_____

The best part of today was...

_____

_____

_____

What can I learn from today's experiences?

_____

_____

_____

Tomorrow I'm looking forward to...

_____

_____

_____

Stop now. Enjoy the moment. It's now
or never.
~Maxime Lagacé

Morning Gratitude

Date: _____

Today I want to feel...

_____

_____

_____

Today I will spread kindness by...

_____

_____

_____

3 things I'm grateful for today are...

_____

_____

_____

Give yourself a gift: the present
moment.
~Marcus Aurelius

To Do List

○ _____
○ _____
○ _____
○ _____
○ _____
○ _____
○ _____
○ _____

Goals

For Tomorrow

Notes

_____
_____
_____
_____
_____

Daily Journal

_____

_____

_____

_____

_____

_____

_____

_____

_____

_____

_____

_____

_____

_____

_____

_____

_____

_____

_____

_____

Evening Gratitude

3 things I'm grateful for today are...

_____
_____
_____

The best part of today was...

_____
_____
_____

What can I learn from today's experiences?

_____
_____
_____

Tomorrow I'm looking forward to...

_____
_____
_____

Whatever the present moment contains,
accept it as if you had chosen it. Always
work with it, not against it.
~Eckhart Tolle

Morning Gratitude

Date: _____

Today I want to feel...

_____

_____

_____

Today I will spread kindness by...

_____

_____

_____

3 things I'm grateful for today are...

_____

_____

_____

Do not dwell in the past. Do not dream
of the future. Concentrate the mind on
the present moment.
~Buddha

To Do List

- ○ _____
- ○ _____
- ○ _____
- ○ _____
- ○ _____
- ○ _____
- ○ _____
- ○ _____

Goals

For Tomorrow

Notes

Daily Journal

_____
_____
_____
_____
_____
_____
_____
_____
_____
_____
_____
_____
_____
_____
_____
_____
_____
_____

Evening Gratitude

3 things I'm grateful for today are...

_____

_____

_____

The best part of today was...

_____

_____

_____

What can I learn from today's experiences?

_____

_____

_____

Tomorrow I'm looking forward to...

_____

_____

_____

A happy man is too satisfied with the
present to dwell too much on the future.
~Albert Einstein

Morning Gratitude

Date: _____

Today I want to feel...

_____

_____

_____

Today I will spread kindness by...

_____

_____

_____

3 things I'm grateful for today are...

_____

_____

_____

The present moment is without
fear or separation.
-Deepak Chopra

Sunday

To Do List

- ○ _____
- ○ _____
- ○ _____
- ○ _____
- ○ _____
- ○ _____
- ○ _____
- ○ _____

Goals

For Tomorrow

Notes

Daily Journal

_____

_____

_____

_____

_____

_____

_____

_____

_____

_____

_____

_____

_____

_____

_____

_____

_____

_____

_____

Evening Gratitude

3 things I'm grateful for today are...

_____

_____

_____

The best part of today was...

_____

_____

_____

What can I learn from today's experiences?

_____

_____

_____

Tomorrow I'm looking forward to...

_____

_____

_____

Anxiety, the illness of our time, comes
primarily from our inability to dwell
in the present moment.
~Thich Nhat Hanh

Weekly check in

DATE _____

TOP 3 THINGS I DID THIS WEEK

- ○ _____
- ○ _____
- ○ _____

THIS WEEK I FELT

NEXT WEEK I WANT TO

_____

_____

_____

_____

MOST REWARDING INTERACTION I HAD THIS WEEK

THINGS I ACCOMPLISHED THIS WEEK

WHAT WAS THE BEST THING ABOUT THE WEEK?

MY RANKING OF THE WEEK

☆ ☆ ☆ ☆ ☆

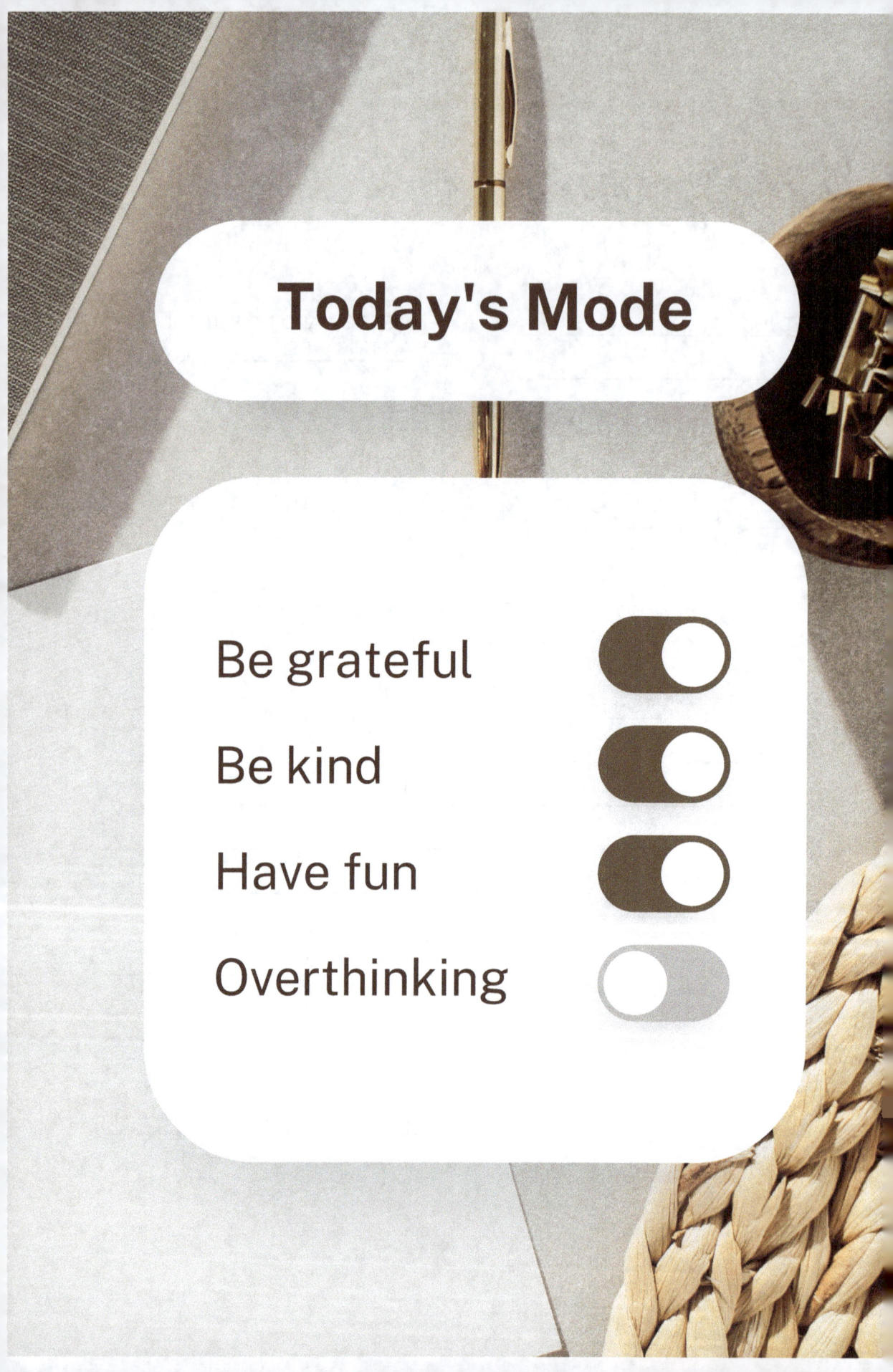

Morning Gratitude

Date: _____

Today I want to feel...

_____

_____

_____

Today I will spread kindness by...

_____

_____

_____

3 things I'm grateful for today are...

_____

_____

_____

Be forgiving with your past self. Be strict
with your present self. Be flexible with
your future self.
-James Clear

To Do List

- ○ _____
- ○ _____
- ○ _____
- ○ _____
- ○ _____
- ○ _____
- ○ _____
- ○ _____

Goals

For Tomorrow

Notes

Daily Journal

Evening Gratitude

3 things I'm grateful for today are...

_____

_____

_____

The best part of today was...

_____

_____

_____

What can I learn from today's experiences?

_____

_____

_____

Tomorrow I'm looking forward to...

_____

_____

_____

Remember that man lives only in the present, in this
fleeting instant; all the rest of his life is either past and
gone, or not yet revealed. Short, therefore, is man's life,
and narrow is the corner of the earth wherein he dwells.
~Marcus Aurelius

Morning Gratitude

Date: _____

Today I want to feel...

_____
_____
_____

Today I will spread kindness by...

_____
_____
_____

3 things I'm grateful for today are...

_____
_____
_____

Breathing and smiling is a deep
practice to bring us back to the
present moment.
~Thich Nhat Hanh

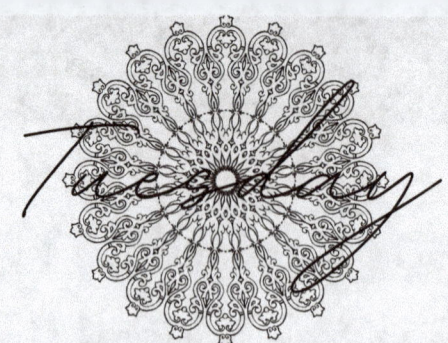

To Do List

- ○ _____
- ○ _____
- ○ _____
- ○ _____
- ○ _____
- ○ _____
- ○ _____
- ○ _____

Goals

For Tomorrow

Notes

_____
_____
_____
_____
_____
_____

Daily Journal

_____

_____

_____

_____

_____

_____

_____

_____

_____

_____

_____

_____

_____

_____

_____

_____

_____

_____

_____

_____

_____

_____

Evening Gratitude

3 things I'm grateful for today are...

_____

_____

_____

The best part of today was...

_____

_____

_____

What can I learn from today's experiences?

_____

_____

_____

Tomorrow I'm looking forward to...

_____

_____

_____

The most important reason to live in the moment is
nothing lasts forever. Enjoy the moment while it's in
front of you; be present. Accept life for what it is – a
finite span of time with infinite possibilities.
~Joshua Fields Millburn

Morning Gratitude

Date: _____

Today I want to feel...

_____
_____
_____

Today I will spread kindness by...

_____
_____
_____

3 things I'm grateful for today are...

_____
_____
_____

If you make friends with the present moment,
and always say 'yes' to whatever is, life becomes
friendly towards you. Life always shows you the
face that you show it. It's always a mirror.
~Eckhart Tolle

Wednesday

To Do List

- ○ _____
- ○ _____
- ○ _____
- ○ _____
- ○ _____
- ○ _____
- ○ _____
- ○ _____

Goals

For Tomorrow

Notes

_____
_____
_____
_____
_____
_____

Daily Journal

_____

_____

_____

_____

_____

_____

_____

_____

_____

_____

_____

_____

_____

_____

_____

_____

_____

_____

_____

_____

_____

Evening Gratitude

3 things I'm grateful for today are...

_____

_____

_____

The best part of today was...

_____

_____

_____

What can I learn from today's experiences?

_____

_____

_____

Tomorrow I'm looking forward to...

_____

_____

_____

Sit just to enjoy your sitting; you don't need to attain
any goal. Each moment of sitting meditation
brings you back to life.
-Thich Nhat Hanh

Morning Gratitude

Date: _____

Today I want to feel...

_____

_____

_____

Today I will spread kindness by...

_____

_____

_____

3 things I'm grateful for today are...

_____

_____

_____

Have patience. All things are difficult
before they become easy.
~Saadi

To Do List

- ○ _____
- ○ _____
- ○ _____
- ○ _____
- ○ _____
- ○ _____
- ○ _____
- ○ _____

Goals

For Tomorrow

Notes

_____
_____
_____
_____
_____
_____

Daily Journal

_____
_____
_____
_____
_____
_____
_____
_____
_____
_____
_____
_____
_____
_____
_____
_____
_____
_____
_____
_____
_____

Evening Gratitude

3 things I'm grateful for today are...

_____

_____

_____

The best part of today was...

_____

_____

_____

What can I learn from today's experiences?

_____

_____

_____

Tomorrow I'm looking forward to...

_____

_____

_____

What lies behind us and what lies before us are
small matters compared to what lies within us.
~Ralph Waldo Emerson

Morning Gratitude

Date: _____

Today I want to feel...

_____
_____
_____

Today I will spread kindness by...

_____
_____
_____

3 things I'm grateful for today are...

_____
_____
_____

Expecting is the greatest impediment to living. In anticipation of tomorrow, it loses today.
~Seneca

To Do List

- _____
- _____
- _____
- _____
- _____
- _____
- _____
- _____

Goals

For Tomorrow

Notes

_____
_____
_____
_____
_____
_____

Daily Journal

_____
_____
_____
_____
_____
_____
_____
_____
_____
_____
_____
_____
_____
_____
_____
_____
_____
_____
_____
_____
_____

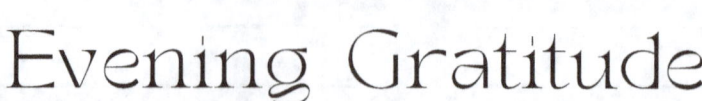

Evening Gratitude

3 things I'm grateful for today are...

_____
_____
_____

The best part of today was...

_____
_____
_____

What can I learn from today's experiences?

_____
_____
_____

Tomorrow I'm looking forward to...

_____
_____
_____

Touch the earth, love the earth, honour the earth,
her plains, her valleys, her hills, and her seas; rest
your spirit in her solitary places.
-Ernest Dimnet

Morning Gratitude

Date: _____

Today I want to feel...

_____

_____

_____

Today I will spread kindness by...

_____

_____

_____

3 things I'm grateful for today are...

_____

_____

_____

Flow with whatever may happen and let your
mind be free. Stay centered by accepting
whatever you are doing. This is the ultimate.
-Zhuangzi

To Do List

- _____
- _____
- _____
- _____
- _____
- _____
- _____
- _____

Goals

For Tomorrow

Notes

Daily Journal

_____

_____

_____

_____

_____

_____

_____

_____

_____

_____

_____

_____

_____

_____

_____

_____

_____

_____

Evening Gratitude

3 things I'm grateful for today are...

_____

_____

_____

The best part of today was...

_____

_____

_____

What can I learn from today's experiences?

_____

_____

_____

Tomorrow I'm looking forward to...

_____

_____

_____

Do not lose your inward peace for anything
whatsoever, even if your whole world seems
upset.
~St. Francis de Sales

Morning Gratitude

Date: _____

Today I want to feel...

_____

_____

_____

Today I will spread kindness by...

_____

_____

_____

3 things I'm grateful for today are...

_____

_____

_____

Preoccupied with a single leaf, you won't see
the tree. Preoccupied with a single tree, you'll
miss the entire forest.
-Takuan

To Do List

- ○ _____
- ○ _____
- ○ _____
- ○ _____
- ○ _____
- ○ _____
- ○ _____
- ○ _____

Goals

For Tomorrow

Notes

Daily Journal

_____
_____
_____
_____
_____
_____
_____
_____
_____
_____
_____
_____
_____
_____
_____
_____
_____
_____
_____
_____
_____

Evening Gratitude

3 things I'm grateful for today are...

_____

_____

_____

The best part of today was...

_____

_____

_____

What can I learn from today's experiences?

_____

_____

_____

Tomorrow I'm looking forward to...

_____

_____

_____

Happiness is not something ready made. It
comes from your own actions.
-Dalai Lama

Weekly check in

DATE _____

TOP 3 THINGS I DID THIS WEEK

○ _____

○ _____

○ _____

THIS WEEK I FELT

NEXT WEEK I WANT TO

_____

_____

_____

_____

MOST REWARDING INTERACTION I HAD THIS WEEK

THINGS I ACCOMPLISHED THIS WEEK

WHAT WAS THE BEST THING ABOUT THE WEEK?

MY RANKING OF THE WEEK

☆ ☆ ☆ ☆ ☆

a beautiful day
begins with
a beautiful mindset

I hope you enjoyed your journey.
Remember, happiness will never dull wi
gratitude in your heart.
~Melissa Eveland

THANK YOU

www.ingramcontent.com/pod-product-compliance
Lightning Source LLC
Chambersburg PA
CBHW081000120626
46546CB00010B/2974